ZPL

I SPY
THANKSGIVING

For Owen Samuel Bernstein
and Kei Scarlett Bernstein,
and with thanks to Dave and Dan
—J.M.

For Robert Word
—W.W.

Text copyright © 2010 by Jean Marzollo. Cover illustration (and first spread) "Into the Woods" from I Spy Fantasy © 1994 by Walter Wick; "A Is for. . ." from I Spy School Days © 1995 by Walter Wick; "Shelter from the Storm" from I Spy Treasure Hunt © 1999 by Walter Wick; "Tiny Toys" from I Spy: A Book of Picture Riddles © 1992 by Walter Wick; "Santa's Workshop" from I Spy Christmas © 1992 by Walter Wick; "A Is for. . ." from I Spy School Days © 1995 by Walter Wick; "Bulletin Board" from I Spy: A Book of Picture Riddles © 1992 by Walter Wick; "1, 2, 3. . ." from I Spy School Days © 1995 by Walter Wick; "A Whale of a Tale" from I Spy Mystery © 1993 by Walter Wick; "Bulletin Board" from I Spy: A Book of Picture Riddles © 1992 by Walter Wick.

All rights reserved. Published by Scholastic Inc.
SCHOLASTIC, CARTWHEEL BOOKS, and associated logos
are trademarks and/or registered trademarks of Scholastic Inc.
Lexile is a registered trademark of MetaMetrics, Inc.

Library of Congress Cataloging-in-Publication Data is available.

ISBN 978-0-545-22094-1

10 9 8 7 6 5 4 3 2   10 11 12 13 14 15
Printed in the U.S.A. 40 • First printing, November 2010

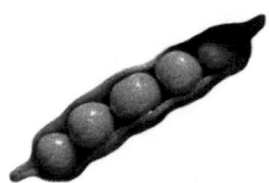

I SPY

THANKSGIVING

Riddles by Jean Marzollo
Photographs by Walter Wick

SCHOLASTIC INC.

New York   Toronto   London   Auckland
Sydney   Mexico City   New Delhi   Hong Kong

I spy

a drum,

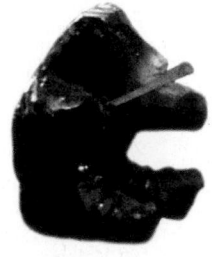

a musical bear,

a table being set,

and a frog in a chair.

I spy

an apple pie,

 a van,

two fish,

 a pumpkin,

and a watering can.

I spy

 a lantern,

the cap of a jar,

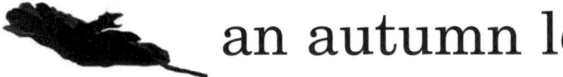 an autumn leaf,

and a lighthouse afar.

I spy

 a little blue mouse,

a 3,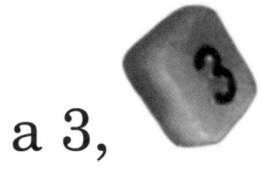

 a baby duck,

a boat,

and a T.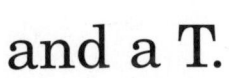

I spy

a Thanksgiving bird,

a bear,

a truck,

a red house,

and an empty chair.